J
9.2
Fen

Kangaroos
and Other Marsupials

Concept and Product Development: Editorial Options, Inc.
Series Designer: Karen Donica
Book Author: Julie A. Fenton

**For information on sales to schools and libraries
in the United States, call 1-800-975-3250.**

**For information on sales to schools and libraries
in Canada, call 1-800-837-5365.**

World Book, Inc.
233 N. Michigan Ave.
Chicago, IL 60601

Library of Congress Cataloging-in-Publication Data

Fenton, Julie A.
    Kangaroos and other marsupials / [book author, Julie A. Fenton].
       p. cm.—(World Book's animals of the world)
    Summary: Questions and answers explore the world of marsupials, animals with pouches, with
an emphasis on the kangaroo.
    ISBN 0-7166-1201-1 -- ISBN 0-7166-1200-3 (set)
    1. Kangaroos—Juvenile literature. 2. Marsupialia—Juvenile literature [1. Kangaroos—
Miscellanea. 2. Marsupials—Miscellanea. 3. Questions and answers.] I. World Book, Inc. II. Title.
III. Series.
    QL737.M35 F46 2000
    599.2—dc21   99-098176

Printed in Singapore

1 2 3 4 5 6 7 8 9 05 04 03 02 01 00

World Book's Animals of the World

Kangaroos
and Other Marsupials

Where is my favorite hiding spot?

World Book, Inc.
A Scott Fetzer Company
Chicago

Contents

Why do I smell like some kinds of cough drops?

Why don't I like my veggies?

How did I get my name?

What Is a Marsupial?

A kangaroo is a marsupial *(mahr SOO pee uhl).* So is a koala. Possums and quokkas are marsupials, too. Marsupial comes from a Latin word meaning pouch.

All marsupials are mammals. Mammals are warm-blooded animals whose young feed on the mother's milk. Marsupials are special kinds of mammals. Most female marsupials have pocketlike pouches on the undersides of their bodies. The pouch acts like a built-in nursery.

Here you see a female kangaroo with her baby. The baby, called a joey, lives in its mother's pouch. The pouch is a safe place for the joey to grow.

Mother and joey

Where in the World Do Marsupials Live?

Millions of years ago, the marsupials lived on one huge continent. Over time, the large continent broke into smaller pieces. The marsupials remained on only two of the pieces—the two that are now South America and Australia. Over time, some of the South American marsupials moved north to live in North America. Many of the American marsupials have died out. Only opossums now live in the Americas.

Most marsupials live in Australia and on nearby islands. Australia is an island continent in the Southern Hemisphere. Australia is surrounded by water on all sides. It has about 150 different kinds of marsupials. These include kangaroos, wallabies, koalas, wombats, and Tasmanian devils. These marsupials do not live anywhere else in the wild. Australia has the most marsupials, but not so many as it once had.

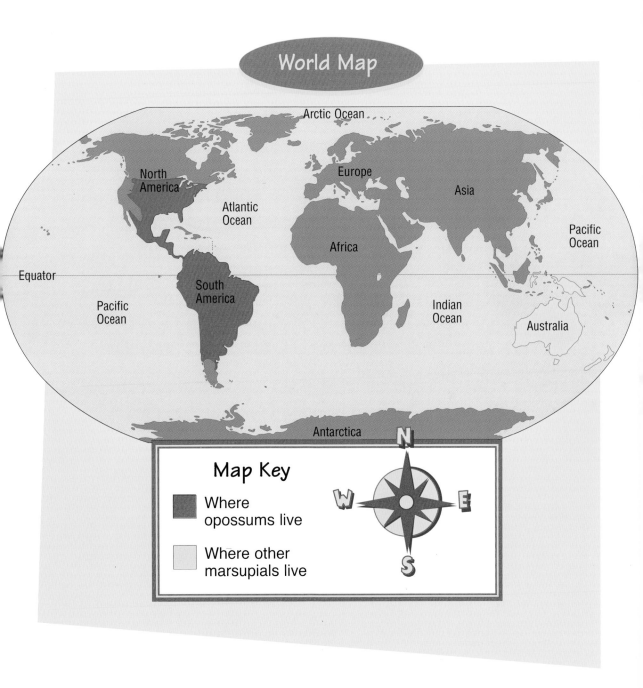

World Map

Arctic Ocean

North America

Europe

Asia

Atlantic Ocean

Pacific Ocean

Africa

Equator

South America

Pacific Ocean

Indian Ocean

Australia

Antarctica

Map Key

Where opossums live

Where other marsupials live

N
W
E
S

Are There Different Types of Kangaroos?

Yes, there are many types of kangaroos. The two main types are red kangaroos and gray kangaroos. Red kangaroos are the largest marsupials in the world. The males have bright coats of thick, red fur. Females are slightly smaller than the adult males. Their coats have some red, but they are mostly smoky blue. As you might have guessed, gray kangaroos have gray fur. Sometimes it looks more like silver. Of all the marsupials, kangaroos have the largest pouches.

Kangaroos have small, furry heads and pointed snouts. They can turn their long ears from front to back to follow sounds. This helps them listen for danger.

Kangaroos have huge back feet and tiny front feet. It's not easy for them to move those huge back legs and feet one at a time. So, they don't run on all four legs the way most animals do. Instead, they run by hopping around, using both of their powerful hind legs and feet.

Red kangaroo

Where Can You Spot Kangaroos?

Kangaroos are grazing animals. They eat grass and other small plants. Kangaroos usually gather in groups, or "mobs," of up to a hundred animals. They live in many habitats, such as woodlands and grasslands. They can also be spotted on rocky hills, in deserts, and even in trees!

Kangaroos are most active at night or early in the day. During the middle of the day, they rest under shady trees or bushes to stay cool.

Most people don't think of kangaroos as tree climbers. But one kind enjoys living the high life. Tree kangaroos have smaller hind feet and bigger front feet than other kangaroos. A tree kangaroo is the only kind of kangaroo that can move one back leg at a time. This lets it walk along branches of trees, where it feeds on leaves or fruit. Sometimes a tree kangaroo jumps to the ground from the treetops. To get back into the tree, it jumps up about 20 feet (6.1 meters).

Tree kangaroo

How Far Can Kangaroos Hop?

Kangaroos are great hoppers. They do more than little bunny hops. Since kangaroos use their powerful hind legs and long feet to hop, their "hops" are more like "jumps." They can hop fast and far.

One hop can carry a kangaroo three or four times its own length. The longest hop recorded is 43 feet (13.1 meters). Kangaroos can travel up to 30 miles (48.3 kilometers) an hour, but they cannot keep that speed up for too long.

When a kangaroo is not hopping, it rests on its big, long tail. The kangaroo uses its tail for pushing off. Its tail helps the kangaroo keep its balance, too.

Red kangaroo

What Do the Bare Bones Show?

If you could see inside a kangaroo's body, here is how its bones would look. Notice how much bigger its hind legs are than its front legs. Its small front legs are used to pull leaves from small plants or to dig into the ground for water. A kangaroo's hind legs are very strong. They help a kangaroo push its entire body off the ground and into the air. These powerful legs allow the kangaroo to hop over objects equal to its own height!

Kangaroos are gentle animals. But if a kangaroo feels threatened, it uses its hind legs to defend itself. The kangaroo leans back on its long tail and strikes the enemy with its strong hind legs and sharp toenails. A single kangaroo kick can cause great harm to an enemy.

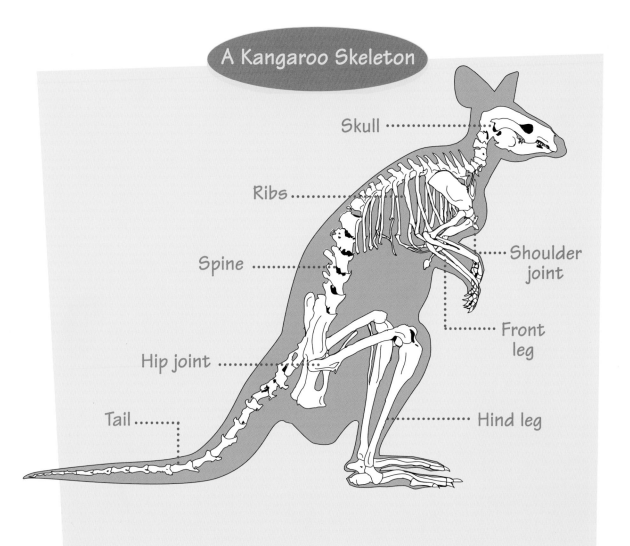

A Kangaroo Skeleton

Skull

Ribs

Spine

Shoulder joint

Front leg

Hip joint

Tail

Hind leg

How Big Is a Joey at Birth?

A female kangaroo gives birth to a joey one month after mating. She raises it alone. A newborn joey doesn't even look like a kangaroo. At birth, the joey is the size of a lima bean. Its body is mostly head and torso. It has no fur, and it cannot see or hear.

Newborn joey

Lima bean

Right after birth, the joey crawls blindly into its mother's pouch. It attaches itself to a teat and begins to drink its mother's milk. The pouch is lined with fur. It's a warm and cozy place to grow. The baby could not survive outside the pouch.

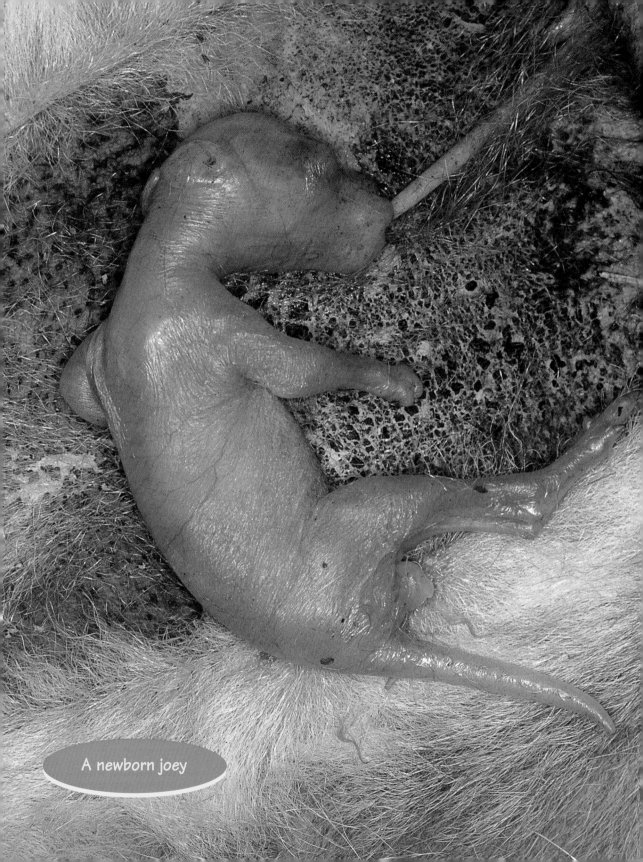

A newborn joey

When Does a Joey Leave the Pouch?

By the time it is 5 months old, a joey finally looks like a kangaroo. Now it begins to take care of itself. The joey learns to find its own food. At first, it leaves its mother's pouch only for short periods. But if something frightens the joey, it hops right back into the pouch.

The joey enters the mother's pouch head first, almost as if it's doing a somersault. Once inside its mother's pouch, the joey turns around. Then it pops its head out of the opening. Mom's pouch is a safe place to hide!

A joey stays close to its mother until it is 2 or 3 years old. The joey continues to drink its mother's milk until it is fully grown.

Gray kangaroo and joey

Is a Wallaby a Kangaroo "Wannabe"?

Well, kind of! This "wannabe" is actually a wallaby. Wallabies are part of the same marsupial family as kangaroos. They are all known as macropods. The word macropod means big foot. Wallabies look just like kangaroos, but most of them have smaller bodies and feet.

A rock wallaby hops among the rocks. Rock wallabies have thick, rough pads on the bottoms of their feet. These pads are just like the soles on hiking shoes. The pads protect rock wallabies' feet and help them grip hard, jagged rocks. Rock wallabies can hop from rock to rock without getting sore feet!

Rock wallaby

How Do Kangaroos Size Up?

The kangaroos of Australia come in all different shapes and sizes. Some are very small. Rat kangaroos are the smallest. A full-grown rat kangaroo is smaller than a rabbit. It stands about a foot tall (30 centimeters). Then come the wallabies. Wallabies range in size from 1 to 6 feet (30 to 180 centimeters). Next come the wallaroos. The biggest family members are the red and gray kangaroos.

The red and gray kangaroos are the heaviest, strongest, and tallest marsupials. A red kangaroo can grow taller than any other kangaroo. "Big red" can grow to be 6 feet (1.8 meters) tall!

Comparison Chart

Height in Feet

7 feet -

6 feet -

5 feet -

4 feet -

3 feet -

2 feet -

1 foot

| Rat Kangaroo | Wallaby | Wallaroo | Red Kangaroo |

What Are Potoroos and Quokkas?

The potoroo *(POH toh roo)* is Australia's most ancient kind of kangaroo. Potoroos have been around for millions of years. They look like tiny rats. A potoroo is less than 10 inches (25 centimeters) tall. It has dark, grayish-brown fur; a pointed snout; and short, round ears. Potoroos dig for food with their front claws. They hop along the ground and feed on roots, mushrooms, and insects.

Another unusual marsupial is the quokka *(KWAH kuh)*. It is one of the smallest kangaroos. It is less than 2 feet (60 centimeters) tall. Quokkas are shy animals that also look like rats. Most quokkas live on Rottnest Island, off the southwest coast of Australia. *Rottnest* is Dutch for *rat's nest*. Rottnest Island was so named because explorers thought quokkas were giant rats.

26

Potoroo

How Did the Wallaroo Get Its Name?

Another type of kangaroo is the wallaroo *(WAHL uh`roo)*, also called the Euro. The name wallaroo is a combination of **walla**by and kanga**roo**. Wallaroos are larger than wallabies and smaller than gray and red kangaroos. Don't let their short legs fool you. Their legs may be short, but they are sturdier than the legs of even the biggest kangaroos. Wallaroos are the only kangaroos with bare, black snouts.

You probably won't see a wallaroo on a hot, sunny day. That's because wallaroos stay "indoors." Like other marsupials, wallaroos conserve body fluids by staying in the shade. But wallaroos find their shade in caves and under rock ledges in hilly areas. When a wallaroo gets thirsty, it doesn't go out looking for a drink. It just digs a water hole in the ground. Now that's creative!

Wallaroo

29

Which Marsupial Looks Like a Bear?

The koala *(koh AH luh)* looks like a teddy bear, but it is not a bear at all. Koalas are marsupials. Like kangaroos, female koalas have pouches where young koalas feed and grow. Unlike kangaroos, however, koalas have pouches that open to the rear of the body. Special muscles around the opening of the pouch can be closed to hold a baby inside. This way, young koalas remain safe as their mothers move around.

Koala mothers and their young enjoy a close relationship. A baby koala lives in its mother's pouch for about seven months. Then it rides on its mother's back for the next six months. The baby koala even sleeps in this "piggyback" position! If a baby koala gets separated from its mother, it will give a loud cry. The baby will cry until it is reunited with its mother.

Koala and baby

Where Do Koalas Hang Out?

During most of the day, a koala sleeps high up in the fork of a eucalyptus tree. The koala spreads its toes and grasps the sides of the tree. Its strong legs and sharp claws help it tightly grasp the trunk.

When the koala moves to a different tree, it usually climbs down to the ground first. Then the koala climbs up the trunk of a nearby tree. The koala may also jump from tree to tree if the forest is thick and the trees are close together.

Koalas rarely drink water. The name koala means no drink in the native Australian language.

Koala

Which Marsupial Lives in North America?

Only one kind of marsupial lives in the wild in North America. That's the common opossum *(uh PAHS uhm)*, also called the Virginia opossum. Millions of years ago, this opossum traveled north from South America.

The tail is very important to the opossum! Its long, scaly tail acts as a fifth hand. The opossum wraps its tail around a tree branch and uses its free hands to grab nearby branches. Its tail is called a prehensile tail. The tail has adapted for grasping and holding on.

Common opossum

How Many Hands Does an Opossum Have?

All four of an opossum's feet work like hands. A young opossum can even hang by its tail and use all four "hands" at once! How do opossums do this?

Well, you can use your thumb to touch any of your other fingers, right? Imagine if you could do the same thing with your big toe. An opossum can! On its hind foot, an opossum has an inside toe that bends like a thumb. It can touch any other toe.

Having feet that work like hands is especially helpful for climbing trees. An opossum can tightly grip branches while climbing to the treetops.

Older, heavier opossums cannot hang upside down. They would fall right out of the tree. Ouch!

Common opossum

How Big Is a Baby Opossum?

A baby opossum is less than a 1/2 inch (13 millimeters) long. That's tinier than a honey bee. A whole litter of opossums can fit in the palm of your hand! A female opossum can give birth to as many as 20 babies at one time. (A kangaroo usually has only 1 baby at a time.)

A female opossum has her first litter in early spring. Before she gives birth, she builds a warm, cozy den. The opossum moves into a burrow abandoned by an animal or into a hollow tree. She fills the den with many layers of leaves and twigs.

The female uses her tail to carry the leaves back to the den. First, she gathers the leaves with her teeth. Then she uses her front legs to pass the leaves to her hind legs. Using her hind legs, she tucks the leaves into a loop that she has made with her tail.

Opossum and babies

What Does It Mean to "Play 'Possum"?

Have you ever kept very still and pretended to be asleep when you really weren't? You were "playing 'possum." The opossum uses this trick, too.

When an opossum faces an enemy, it pretends to be dead. The opossum closes its eyes, or it stares without blinking. Its tongue may even hang out of its mouth. The opossum will remain motionless even if an enemy tosses it about.

The opossum can lie perfectly still for up to six hours. Most animals won't try to eat another animal if they think it's dead. When the enemy goes away, the opossum rolls over, gets up, and walks away.

Opossum

Opossum or Possum— Is There a Difference?

James Cook, an English explorer, first visited Australia in 1770. This explorer saw a furry little animal that lived in trees. It had a gripping tail and a pouch on its belly.

This furry creature reminded the explorer of the American animal called the opossum. So he gave the same name to the Australian animal. But these two marsupials were not closely related. The name "opossum" was shortened to "possum" *(PAHS uhm)* to tell it apart from the American animal. Possums, not to be mistaken for opossums, are marsupials that live in Australia and nearby islands.

Here you see a brush-tailed possum from Australia. It's about the size of a cat. It has a beautiful coat that comes in silver-gray, black, or reddish-brown. It can live in many places, but it likes the forest best because it can rest in tree hollows there.

Brush-tailed possum

Can a Possum Fly?

One kind of possum can fly—in a way. The sugar glider is a member of one of the most unusual marsupial families. It is a gliding possum, or glider. This marsupial lives in trees. It doesn't have wings, so it can't really fly. But it can glide long distances.

The glider has a fold of skin that joins its front and rear legs on each side of its body. These furry folds act like wings. When the animal spreads its front and rear legs, it can glide from branch to branch. Some gliders can sail as far as 350 feet (107 meters) in one glide. That's farther than the length of an American football field!

Sugar glider

Do Possums or Opossums Make Good Pets?

Just a few kinds of both animals can be good pets. The sugar glider is one kind of possum that can be a pet. It is easily tamed. The sugar glider got its name because it has a sweet tooth. It likes the sweet nectar of flowers.

One kind of opossum that makes a good pet is the short-tailed opossum. It looks like a cute mouse. It is usually found in South America. Short-tailed opossums have short, thick fur. Nice and cuddly! They help get rid of pests around the house because they love to eat insects and baby mice.

Most other kinds of possums and opossums are not so friendly to people. They prefer to live on their own. They nest in trees or bush areas. They eat fruit, flower blossoms, and insects.

Short-tailed opossum

Where Do Tasmanian Devils Hide Out?

Tasmanian *(taz MAY nee uhn)* devils are found only on the Australian island of Tasmania. They live in many places on the island, but they like the forests best. If you turn over a large stone or look in an old tree stump, you may find a Tasmanian devil's home, which is called a den.

Tasmanian devils are small, short-legged animals. They look like black bear cubs. They have shaggy black fur, sharp claws, and very powerful jaws and teeth. These marsupials look devilish because they are fierce and noisy, but they make noise mostly out of fear.

Some marsupials are carnivores *(KAHR nuh vawrs)*. Carnivores do not like most plants. They eat mainly meat. Tasmanian devils are meat-eating marsupials. They feed on small marsupials and reptiles, plus any dead animals they can find. Tasmanian devils hunt mainly at night.

Tasmanian devil

Do Tasmanian Devils Throw Tantrums?

Tasmanian devils have very bad tempers. They whirl back and forth when they are angry. These little marsupials jump from side to side so fast that they are hard to see.

The Tasmanian devil is a loudmouth, too! Its weird sound goes from a soft bark or snort, to a loud snarl, and then to a really loud scream. It can be heard from over a mile away.

If you saw a Tasmanian devil throwing a tantrum, you might be frightened. Its wild behavior scares many people. But in spite of its bad temper, Tasmanian devils would rather hide from an enemy than fight one!

Tasmanian devil

Which Marsupial Is an Expert Tunnel-Digger?

Wombats have large, chubby bodies and short legs. They have sharp claws on their front feet that are great for digging. Wombats live in burrows under the ground. They dig tunnels with their front feet and push the soil out of the way with their hind feet. Some wombat burrow systems have measured more than 100 feet (30 meters) in length!

Wombats are very shy animals. In fact, they like to hide. They spend most of their time in tunnels underground.

Like koalas and many other marsupials, wombats have pouches that open to the rear of the body. This way, mother wombats can dig without getting soil in their pouches!

Wombat

Do Bandicoots Have Long or Short Noses?

It depends on the bandicoot *(BAN duh koot)*! Most types of this ratlike animal have long pointed snouts. But one type has a nose that is short. It is called, of course, the short-nosed bandicoot.

The bandicoot is another marsupial with a backward-opening pouch. All bandicoots have sharp teeth and strong claws. At night, bandicoots use their noses and claws to dig up earthworms, insects, bulbs, and plant roots.

The eastern barred bandicoot has a beautiful coat. Its shiny fur is grayish-brown on top and creamy-white on the belly, feet, and thin tail. The eastern barred bandicoot has pale stripes, or bars, across its hindquarters. That is how it gets its name.

Eastern barred bandicoot

57

When Is It Time to Move Out?

Bandicoots are the fastest breeders of all mammals. Their young are born 12 ½ days after mating. And a new litter may be born before the last litter leaves its mother's pouch. If the pouch gets too crowded, the older bandicoots leave the pouch. They are able to survive on their own outside the pouch.

As soon as the older bandicoots move out, each newborn baby fastens its mouth to a teat in the mother's pouch. The baby is too little to hold onto the teat by itself. The teat swells inside the baby's mouth. This keeps the baby from falling off. The baby stays nice and secure in the pouch. When the young bandicoot is big enough, it drops off the teat. Now it is time to move out.

Rabbit-eared bandicoot

Are Marsupials in Danger?

In Australia, many marsupials are in danger of becoming extinct. People have brought foxes and wild dogs to Australia. These animals prey upon the marsupials. In clearing land for farms and cities, people have destroyed the marsupials' homes and their food sources.

Human hunters have killed many of these animals for their soft, beautiful fur. The koala was almost wiped out, but now special laws protect this marsupial. Koalas are very lucky to have gotten a second chance!

People in Australia are working to protect other marsupials, too.

Koala

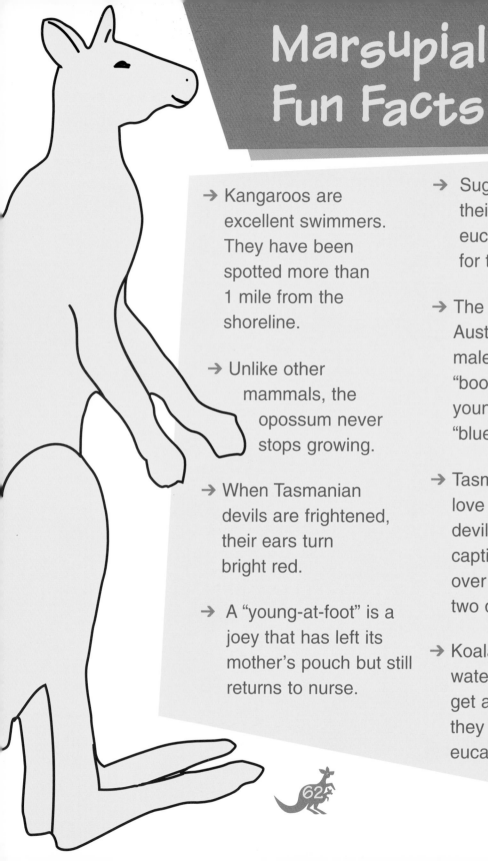

Marsupial Fun Facts

→ Kangaroos are excellent swimmers. They have been spotted more than 1 mile from the shoreline.

→ Unlike other mammals, the opossum never stops growing.

→ When Tasmanian devils are frightened, their ears turn bright red.

→ A "young-at-foot" is a joey that has left its mother's pouch but still returns to nurse.

→ Sugar gliders use their teeth to tap eucalyptus trees for their sap.

→ The people of Australia call adult male kangaroos "boomers." They call young females "blue fliers."

→ Tasmanian devils love food. One devil escaped from captivity and ate over 50 chickens in two days.

→ Koalas rarely drink water because they get all the liquid they need from eucalyptus leaves.

Glossary

breed To produce young.

carnivore An animal that eats mostly meat.

den An animal's home.

eucalyptus A tree found in Australia.

extinct Died out and never seen again.

habitat The area where an animal lives, such as grasslands or desert.

joey A baby marsupial, especially a baby kangaroo.

litter Young produced by an animal at one birth.

mammal A warm-blooded animal that feeds its young on the mother's milk.

marsupial A mammal whose young are not fully developed at birth. The newborn grows in its mother's pouch.

mob A group of marsupials, especially kangaroos.

pouch The pocket of skin where a female marsupial carries her young until it is fully developed.

prehensile Capable of grasping and holding by wrapping around.

teat The part of a mother's body through which the baby feeds on her milk.

torso The body except for the head, arms, and legs.

Index

(**Boldface** indicates a photo, map, or illustration.)

Picture Acknowledgments: Cover: © Bill Bachman, Photo Researchers; © Brian Parker, Tom Stack & Associates; © Kenneth W. Fink, Bruce Coleman Inc.; © Erwin & Peggy Bauer, Bruce Coleman Collection; © Jen & Des Bartlett, Bruce Coleman Inc. Back Cover: © Norman O. Tomalin, Bruce Coleman Inc.; © Ken Stepnell, Bruce Coleman Inc.; © Dave Watts, Tom Stack & Associates; © Tom McHugh, Photo Researchers; © Bill Bachman, Photo Researchers 3; © Jen & Des Bartlett, Bruce Coleman Inc. 45; © Erwin & Peggy Bauer, Bruce Coleman Collection 37; © Erwin & Peggy Bauer, Bruce Coleman Collection 4, 51; © John Cancalosi, Bruce Coleman Collection. 31, 35; © Jean-Paul Ferrero, AUSCAPE 5, 47; © Kenneth W. Fink, Bruce Coleman Inc. 13; © Thomas Kitchin, Tom Stack & Associates 29; © Jeff Lepore, Photo Researchers 39; © Tom McHugh, Photo Researchers 49, 59; © Brian Parker, Tom Stack & Associates 61; © M.R. Phicton, Bruce Coleman Collection 19; © Hans Reinhard, Bruce Coleman Inc. 4, 7, 21, 33; © Leonard Lee Rue, Bruce Coleman Collection 41; © David M. Schleser, Photo Researchers 43; © Ken Stepnell, Bruce Coleman Inc. 27; © Norman O. Tomalin, Bruce Coleman Inc. 15, 23; © Dave Watts, Tom Stack & Associates 11, 53, 55, 57.
Illustrations: WORLD BOOK illustration by Michael DiGiorgio 17, 25; WORLD BOOK illustration by Karen Donica 9, 62